Love Distortion

BELLE, BATTERED CODEPENDENT & OTHER LOVE STORIES

BY Tracee Sioux

Dedicated to Jeremy, Ainsley and Zack,
who teach me what Authentic Love is.
Also, to all mothers and fathers who want
Authentic Love for their daughters and sons.

CHAPTERS

The Conception of The Girl Revolution

In 2006, when my daughter, Ainsley, was around four years old, I, with the new perspective of being a mother instead of a daughter or an independent woman of the late twentieth century, began to look at media, stories and messages about femininity differently.

I became concerned with the Love Stories we tell our girls and began to correlate them to real world problems in our culture, like rape and relationship violence. I explored the correlations on my blog, *The Girl Revolution*, TheGirlRevolution.com (known formerly as *So Sioux Me: Empowering Girls*).

My interest in this was personal and parental; I did not want to pass on the disastrous Love Distortions of my own romantic past. It was also as an advocate for the female gender; don't we all want to know what Authentic Love is and to help each other get there by examining the pitfalls of our traditional and cultural love stories and writing new, healthier ones for ourselves and for our daughters?

The first part of the book is Disney heavy. Disney tells many of the Love Stories girls grow up on, not just about love but about other aspects of life as well. Not every Disney product is as bad as others are. Because Disney tells so many of our girl stories, I think their product line deserves examination. Not every post is about negative Love Stories. There are brilliant works. I, personally, thought Disney's *Tangled* was a well-told story and its love messaging was more appropriate than Disney's historical message. One can hope Disney is listening.

These posts have been left largely unedited, and sometimes the posts conflict. The messages to women and girls and about women and girls and love, these messages conflict in our culture. It's difficult to sift through and make sense of it all.

Time elapses over the course of these posts or chapters, and as time elapsed, my feelings and perceptions in some cases changed, shifted or became more clarified. My daughter is now nine and no longer feels compelled to sport a tiara, my fear about the Disney Princess Culture has lessened in direct correlation to its attraction for her.

The posts draw a correlation between the real dating violence in our culture and the love stories our girls grow up on, especially those in popular media. I hope I served the subject matter well.

I hope you enjoy the posts, which can still be found on *The Girl Revolution*, should you wish to make a comment on any of them. I welcome your input. I don't expect all readers to agree with me—these issues are complex, and there are many valid points of view—but I do hope it makes all readers ask themselves some questions about the Love Stories we spoon-feed our girls.

Princess Ban

"No princesses, Bratz or Barbie gifts," read the invitation for my daughter's fifth birthday party this year. The week before we had gone to the used bookstore and sold all my daughter's *Cinderella, Beauty and the Beast, Snow White, Sleeping Beauty, The Little Mermaid* and Barbie books. I allowed her to pick other, healthier books to replace them.

I was bracing myself for a big crying fit when I told her we were banning princesses and Barbie. We had never allowed Bratz— because obviously they look like hoochies, and they are brats, and I certainly don't want her emulating that kind of garbage. But really it was all very easy and calm, and I think she even enjoyed the extra attention given to her girlness and her ideas of girlness.

"We're going to the used bookstore," I told her one morning. "Why don't you gather up all your princess and Barbie books so we can sell them and get other books?"

"Why can't I keep my princess books, Mommy?" she asked.

"Because all those princesses just sit around waiting for a man, the prince, to come save them," I told her. "And you do not need saving. You can wake yourself up, you don't need some guy to show up and kiss you to wake yourself from a nightmare," I said emphatically.

This seemed to make sense to her, as I had already taught her how to wake herself up from a nightmare. "Well, Belle doesn't need a guy to wake her up," she said.

"Belle gets kidnapped, and then she turns the beast into a prince with her love," I explained. "You don't fall in love with someone who kidnaps or traps you; that's called Stockholm Syndrome, and I guarantee that if you marry a beast someday, he will stay a beast and never, ever turn into a prince."

"Ariel doesn't wait for someone to wake her up," she said thoughtfully.

"Worse," I told her. "Ariel gives up her gift of voice and her entire family for the first man she ever sees! You should never give up your gifts to get a man, especially not your voice or your ability to say what you want, and you should never let a man isolate you from your family. You should not marry the first man who likes you; you should date a few more to find out what you want," I responded.

"Cinderella could have rescued herself from her stepmother if she had gotten good grades and had gone to college to be a lawyer or a doctor. Then she wouldn't have had to deal with her stepmother or her stepsisters. She didn't need Prince Charming to find her glass slipper and marry her away from them. She should have saved herself," I said.

"What about Barbie?" she asked.

"Barbie doesn't ever *do* anything," I explained. "She just sits around looking pretty or buying big houses or flashy cars and a bunch of clothes. Really, don't you think there should be more to life than buying stuff? How does Barbie make the world a better place?"

"I don't know," she said.

"Well, I want you to be able to do things for yourself when you grow up," I told her, "so no more princesses or Barbie."

"Okay, but can I keep this one? It has *Alice in Wonderland* in it and other stories, too," she asked.

It was an expensive collection of stories my mother had given her, and I wasn't yet ready to offend my mother by selling her gifts to the used bookstore, so I relented.

And we only had to return one set of princess flash cards on her birthday. After a few tears, she was pretty happy about the paint set she chose instead. And surprisingly, I think she gets it. I think she really does understand that it's important for girls to do stuff and not wait around for boys to come save them. Or at least on some cellular level she gets it, and my struggle will not have been in vain. Now when we go to the store, she just accepts that we don't buy princess stuff, like not being allowed to buy Bratz or Cheetah girls paraphernalia is a rule because they seem to have lost or grown out of all their clothes.

Cinderella Should Have Saved Herself

Our daughters are inundated with Cinderella and her friends. Young girls love Cinderella and want to be her.

For several years I allowed the Cinderella obsession to run rampant. I allowed the dress up clothes, books, movies, birthday party themes, posters, sticker and coloring books, flash cards, and on and on. There seemed to be no end in sight. It was completely against my gut instinct. When I read Ainsley the books or watched the movies, I would cringe inside, my gut kept telling me, "This is so unempowering."

When she was four, I realized these things would not resolve themselves, and the message that she needed "saving" was going to have negative consequences for her life. It would especially effect her love life and her ability to be happily alone or independent.

I told her the truth about Cinderella and banned most paraphernalia. If you critically deconstruct this fairytale, there is nothing harmless about it. It is probably harmless as a simple story, but the degree to which it is marketed to young girls makes it a huge influence in their lives.

Have you ever talked to a young woman, newly engaged and planning her storybook wedding? You realize she's living her Cinderella fantasy, and she truly believes something magical is happening, and she expects to live happily ever after. When I meet these girls, I always feel terribly sympathetic for the truths they will discover in about a year. Wouldn't it be kinder to our daughters if we told them the truth about love and marriage and "the prince"? Wouldn't it be more empowering if their expectations were in line with reality?

So, I told my daughter first that Cinderella didn't need saving. She could have saved herself. At least in today's practical world, the one my daughter relates to, Cinderella had options. She could have graduated from high school and gone off to college. She could have gotten a medical or law degree. She could have left her stepmother's home, achieved an education, then a job. Had she done that, she would have had no need for her stepmother's money.

Cinderella also made a giant mistake by attempting to find "happily ever after" in another person. What she could have done is learned how to make herself happy first. She could have found hobbies and had friends and pursued something. She shouldn't have wasted her life waiting.

On a practical note, Cinderella hated her life because she had to do all the housework. So she became a wife!

Stupid, stupid, stupid. How many women out there got married and then realized how much housework is involved in raising a family? I certainly do a lot of housework as a wife. Most wives I know do most of the housework. If my daughter gets married and expects to do no housework, she'll be severely disappointed.

I'm married. Every married woman knows one basic truth— it's a lot more work than we were told. I think it's a valid and wonderful institution, but it's no quick easy way to happily ever after. My daughter deserves to know that. It's also not the only way for women to find happiness.

I'm no lawyer, but depending on the state she lived in, Cinderella could have just sued her stepmother for her inheritance. I know in Texas the estate is split between the children and the wife if there is no will.

Cinderella is a terrible example of an empowered girl. But she can be used as a good teaching tool. We can point out what she did wrong. We can also offer great alternatives like college and careers, and we can encourage girls to find their own true selves. I think we owe them that.

For better ideas about love and self to give our daughters try these two books: *Princess Bubble*, where she'll learn she can save herself, and *The Missing Piece Meets the Big O*, where she'll learn she is whole and complete already.

Belle: Battered Codependent

By now no one will be surprised when I say that I'm not a huge fan of Belle from Disney's *Beauty and the Beast*.

Some might see Belle as a redeeming character because she is smart and loves to read. She is, after all, bright enough to tell Gaston, the quintessential good-looking football player type, where to go. Good for Belle, even though all the other village girls love Gaston, she thinks he's a moron, and she is looking for something different.

When her mad scientist father gets held as a hostage by the mean, ugly beast, Belle, the loyal daughter, finds him. Selflessly, she trades her own freedom so that her father can go to the invention festival. What?

Here's the first lesson we need to tell our daughters, "Your dad and I will never, ever trade you for anything. If you are ever held by a beast or anyone else, we *will* bring the police and find you or die trying. If you are ever kidnapped or someone tries to take you, then you should do anything you can to get away. Scream, bite, scratch, kick and run as fast as you can.

The rest of the story is basically how Belle is such a good and sweet young woman that she transforms the compassionless, angry, self-absorbed, violent, ugly and mean beast into the prince he always was inside.

Basically, the story is just early training for future battered women everywhere. This is Stockholm Syndrome. Women love to love their abuser and fantasize that eventually she'll love him enough that he'll start treating her with love and respect. Every abused woman desperately wants to believe that her compassionless, angry, mean, self-absorbed jerk of a husband or boyfriend has a kind prince locked inside, and if she is just a good and sweet and forgiving enough wife or girlfriend, then she can change him into a sweet guy.

What kind of codependent crap are we feeding our daughters at bedtime? We're setting them up to be victims with this story. Is it any surprise that 30 percent of women put up with abuse at some point in their lives? Come on!

I recommend telling our daughters the truth.

If you marry a mean and selfish or violent beast of a man, you will never, ever change him into a nice guy. People are who they are. No one has the power to change anyone else. Don't waste your life trying.

The best thing to do is to marry a guy who is already good and sweet and kind and generous. Find someone who treats you with respect from the beginning and skip all the fairytale drama.

Here's the Challenge: add, if not completely replace some of these princess horror stories with stories that have good messages like *The Practical Princess*, and other liberating fairytales. And give your daughters a new perspective on the old messages found in Disney's version.

Ariel:
The Little Mute

My daughter, like every five-year-old girl, loves the Disney Princesses. I mean, we can't really walk through any store without seeing clothing, dolls, books, backpacks, flash cards, puzzles, games, dress up clothes, videos, bedspreads and shoes that are logoed with these princesses.

Since banning the princess paraphernalia, we like to play a little game. She tries to think up a princess who was an empowered girl, and I explain to her why that princess is not an acceptable role model.

"What's wrong with Ariel, The Little Mermaid?" Ainsley asks.

First, Ariel made a deal with the devil. Ursula is pretty much the evil devil character in the story. You must never assume the devil will look a certain way. You should never believe anyone who tells you they can give you something you desire if you give up your talents because most likely they are lying.

Second, Ariel had the gift of a beautiful voice. That's a talent given to her by God. When God gives you a gift or a talent, you don't ever trade that for some guy. I don't care who the guy is. If he loves you, there will be room for your gifts and talents to flourish.

Third, Ariel fell for the first man she saw. Smart girls date and have a few boyfriends before they settle down and get married.

See, it takes practice and trying different boyfriends out before you really know what kind of man will be best for you. Never marry the first man you see.

Fourth, Ariel gave up her family for the prince. True love will never require that you abandon your parents or siblings or friends or life. If a man wants you to give up family or friends to be with him, then he doesn't really love you.

Fifth, Ariel gave up her voice. No man worthy of your love will want you to give up your voice. You have important things to say, valid and worthy things. Any man you marry should encourage you to say what you think and voice your opinions. Don't ever, ever let a man silence you.

Princess Culture Examined

Ever wonder how and why the Disney Princess Culture distorts and minimizes girlness, leaving girls as the token extra character or one that desperately needs to be saved or silenced?

My filmmaker friend, Aaron Lea, sent me this rejection letter to a Mary V. Ford from Disney, dated 1938. It states that she should not bother sending her portfolio because the creative talent is, by company policy, men.

This does help explain how the Disney Princess Girl Culture became so destructive and minimizing to girls.

Dear Miss Ford:

...Women do not do any of the creative work in connection with preparing the cartoons for the screen, as that work is performed entirely by young men. For this reason girls are not considered for the training school.

The only work open to women consists of tracing the characters on clear celluloid sheets with India ink and filling in the tracings on the reverse side with pain, according to directions.

In order to apply for a position as "Inker" or "Painter" it is necessary that one appear at the Studio, bringing samples of pen and ink and watercolor work. It would not be advisable to come to Hollywood with the above specifically in view, as there really are very few openings in comparison with the number of girls who apply.

Yours very truly,

Walt Disney Productions, LTD.

Aaron explained how during World War II, Disney was put in a position, like most companies, to need women artists, which is how one of his creative idols, Mary Blair, was given some creative power.

Mary Blair was an art supervisor and designer at Disney when they were at their highest level of brilliance. Disney optioned to use her artwork for storybook versions of certain films in place of stills.

"Blair's influence can still be found today—she inspires a lot of us creative types. The opening credits for *Monsters, Inc.* are definitely homage to her, as well as *Foster's Home for Imaginary Friends*," Lea pointed out.

There is an article In *New York Entertainment*, examining whether things are that much different at Disney in 2008 than they were in 1938. "The *IMDb* credits for Disney's latest No. 1 movie, *Ratatouille*, list twenty-six separate animators—of whom exactly zero appear, based on first names, to be women," they cite. Two female story participants were given the glorious titles of "additional story material," indicative of their involvement.

In 2011, Aimee Schribner, a woman, was finally given an associate producer credit for her work on *Tangled*, Disney's version of Rapunzel. Up to this point, the screenplay writers, producers, creative art directors and most other credits have been male. Men are great, but it does make me wonder why, exactly, Disney isn't hiring women to tell stories about what it means to be feminine and desired to girls. I know that it's not a lack of talent or creative genius on the part of women.

Shrek the Third: Princess Confrontation

We took our kids to *Shrek the Third*. I was thrilled to expose the girls to the scene where the Disney Princesses Snow White, Cinderella, and Sleeping Beauty deliberately nod off to sleep to "wait to be rescued" when the villains of children's literature lock them up.

Fiona and her mother look mystified by such a stupid response and take matters into their own hands—effectively saving themselves.

Hello! It's about time someone had the nerve to confront those girls about the stupidity of waiting around for someone to save them. Thank you Fiona and Queen of Far Far Away!

I used to allow princesses at our house; I've since banned them. The messages of the Disney Princess Culture is that girls are valued for beauty rather than competence, that a prince must come save them, for they are incapable of effective action.

If parents are going to offer their daughters the Disney Princess Culture, and it's really not possible to isolate them from it completely because it's so pervasively marketed, they should at least offer up an alternate view of a girl's role. *Shrek the Third* should join the others on the DVD shelf, at the very least. Use it to point out to your daughters the (dis)functionality of the

Disney stories. Give them permission to envision saving themselves and being proactive about their lives.

Tell them the truth about men they will date someday—that prince grows up and turns into a fallible man that picks his nose and turns right back into a frog—just like the King of Far Far Away does in *Shrek The Third.*

Watch *Shrek the Third* and tell her that you think Fiona and her mother's actions are more admirable than the princesses who passively nod off to sleep and wait for someone to save them.

Enchanted: New Generation Princess Fable

Disney's princess tales all attempt to answer one question: What do girls/women want? According to Disney's traditional message to little girls, what women want is to be saved by a prince, fall instantly in love and live happily ever after.

As a woman and a parent, I've been waiting for Disney to come into the new millennium with a more up-to-date, girl-friendly version of its own princess drama. Shrek was great, but it lacked the Disney Magic that makes little girls drool.

Over a rainy weekend my daughter and I rented *Enchanted*, Disney's newest version of its own princess tales.

Enchanted does question the Disney Princess Culture, kinda. Sorta. Maybe.

The evil stepmother still finds the princess threatening and attempts to do away with her by sending her to New York City, "where dreams never come true."

The princess, Giselle, meets a single father who is about to become engaged to the exact opposite of a Disney Princess archetype, Nancy. Nancy is a professional, single woman who acknowledges that she's never had much use for Prince Charming, but she is holding out for a decent guy. A coworker accuses her of being a secret hopeless romantic underneath her practical exterior. The accusation proves true when she gets exhilarated by an uncharacteristic invitation to a ball and nearly swoons over a gift of real flowers instead of the usual e-card.

Our single father, Robert, is a divorce lawyer who was left by the mother of his child, a daughter for whom he buys books like *Great Women in History* instead of the princess book she really wants. Disney pokes a little fun at parents like me, who take issue with the Princess Save Me Culture and wish to present our daughters with a more realistic expectation for their futures. They highlight Madam Curie and point out that she died of radiation poisoning—which isn't as much fun or as magical a story as living happily ever after. Touché, Disney. My daughter wholeheartedly agrees. But is it really more romantic to give up your voice to get a man? Or to fall in love with and try to change your kidnapper?

"Oh, you can try to withhold Princess Culture all you like," Disney seems to challenge, as they have the six-year-old girl jump out of a taxi and chase down our Princess Giselle as she mistakenly tries to enter a billboard in the shape of a castle. She falls right into the arms of our unprincely hero, Robert. He, of course, agrees to help her but not to save her, much to his daughter's chagrin. Very much like the disappointment I'm sure my own daughter feels when I tell her to pick a movie other than *Cinderella* or *Sleeping Beauty* at the video store.

Princess Giselle behaves as a caricature of her own princess self. Basically, she is full of larger-than-life false hand movements and emotional twittering, and she says unbelievably ridiculous things about being saved and the power of true love's kiss. She's incapable of any emotion aside from happiness and joy and goodness. She's naive to the point of being deranged. To its credit, Disney dares to poke as much fun as its own history and its creation of the idiotic lunacy of Princess Culture as it pokes at me for being less than charmed by it.

A shift in Princess Giselle occurs when she and her non-prince savior, Robert, set against the backdrop of street theater in Central Park, begin to discuss dating versus falling-in-love-at-first-sight and what happens after "happily ever after." It seems our princess was previously unaware that she might have job after marriage, and that her job might be part of what makes her happy. She didn't know that she could express her thoughts, dreams and desires to her love-at-first-sight-prince fiancé should he show up to save her.

For his part, our non-princess-saving man realizes that it certainly won't kill him to offer up a little romance to show his practical, modern-day woman, Nancy, that he loves her. (No, I think, it certainly won't kill you to go to a little effort. Maybe I'll send this particular *YouTube* video to my own modern-day, practical man. Hint, hint.)

Giselle experiences anger for the first time when Robert confronts her with the reality that her prince probably isn't coming, and it's time for Plan B. Plan B, in Princess Culture lingo is, I believe, a job or a sense of purpose. Our naive Princess Giselle is seen flipping through *Great Women of History* with a new interest.

Of course, this is a Disney film, so our prince, like many Princes of Romance Past, does arrive to save our princess. And our prince, like many Princes of Romance Past, is a completely self-absorbed dope—cute, but lacking substance. (Who doesn't remember that guy? Luckily, ladies, we skirted that future—by going on a date before it was too late.)

In light of her own personal awakening, our Princess Giselle demands a date before they return to Andalasia. On the date she realizes maybe her love-at-first-sight prince and she don't really have all that much in common. Maybe she's making a terrible mistake? Maybe she loves the man who doesn't want to save her, but who took the time to ask her what she wanted to be when she grew up? Maybe?

The film takes a detour worth looking at. Giselle decides she needs a ball gown, and our six-year-old girl snags Daddy's emergency credit card, with a quip about this being an emergency, and the two jaunt around New York on a spending spree. The little girl precociously fills our naive princess in on today's beauty culture. It seems Disney might be juxtaposing the innocence of their own interpretation of girlness with the current hyper-sexualized, appearance-oriented one. Perhaps they are asking, "How is this better?" The answer: "It's not."

Like Disney Princess Films of generations past we end up at…a ball. Where else?

The evil queen comes to do away with our princess to prevent her from taking over her kingdom, and Giselle takes a bite of her poisoned apple (Oh, Eve, will you ever learn?).

Of course, she's not awakened to our simple-minded, self-absorbed, pretty boy prince. She is awakened to our single father, divorce lawyer prince. His date, Nancy, whom he intended to marry five minutes ago, gives him permission to kiss Giselle, and she does awaken with the words, "I knew it was you." They make a new modern-day family, the father, nice stepmother and daughter (who got a world full of romance and princessness to make her deliriously happy).

Giselle, in a modern-day twist, saves her True Love. Thanks Disney, I've been waiting a long time for that. That is some gender progress.

This leaves our professional Nancy, who realizes she does want to be saved after all and jumps down the rabbit hole/manhole with Prince Charming and Lives "happily ever after" in Andalasia.

In light of yesterday's *The Girl Revolution* story, "Princess Culture Examined," I had to wonder. Whose interpretation of what women want is this? To answer that, I watched the special features on how the magic was made and listened to the interviews with the director, writers, choreographers, sound people, production people, etc. I went to the *IMDb* database and checked the credits of the entire cast and crew.

It was written by a man, directed by a man, and produced by men.

Out of nine listed producers, only one, Jill Morris, is a woman. The music is by a man, as is the cinematography, film editing, art direction, production design and special effects. Out of five, two women are given credit for production management. A woman did the costume design, and one of the two casting credits goes to a woman.

Disney's new updated version of "what women want" is really "men's new interpretation of what women want."

I just have a few questions for Disney: Why is it that you think women aren't capable of telling our own story in your magical universe? Don't you think women might be better witnesses about our own experience and desires than men are?

I would love to see the *female* interpretation of what women want. I want to see Jane interpreted by *Jane*.

Disney, aren't you at all curious to see if you're right?

The Princess and the Frog: Review

I'm torn between whether or not to write a full critique of *The Princess and the Frog*, the way I have for the other films in the Disney Princess Culture. I could, you know, deconstruct the whole thing and look for meaning, obvious and subtle, relate it to the Feminist Promise of the Past and today's Working Mother Reality. I want to at once say this film was accurate in terms of teaching our daughters to dream and warn poor Tiana that dreams get exhausting and perhaps less fulfilling or important when you throw a baby or two into the mix.

And seriously, Tiana, do. not. marry. a. man. who. does. not. see. the. value. of. an. honest. day's. work. A spoiled, poor prince playboy? Oh, my goodness. One could an entire doctoral thesis on today's Hip Hop Pimp culture, current African American demographics and family crises, and the gender/work theme in this film.

But, unlike the rest of the Disney Princess genre this movie just came out.

I don't want to ruin it for you or your children. Really, I don't.

Instead, I'll say "hurray" for Disney. They finally have an African American princess in Tiana.

The plot was fun. The story was creative. The themes and romance were appropriate for children. The cast was darling. It was super-colorful and interesting and fun. The film even poked some fun at its own genre with one character insanely obsessed with marrying a prince at any cost. Its setting is in New Orleans, a town with a rich and colorful heritage that could surely use the boost.

Both my son and daughter enjoyed this film equally, and frankly, so did I.

They don't make a new Disney Princess movie every day. As much fun as it is to deconstruct them, it's equally fun to go see them and experience them with your kids. Disney Princess films are, after all, an integral narrative to our love stories, for better or worse.

CHOOSING PRINCES

I was thinking about what I hate about the Princess Culture. It's for the same reason I hate The Bachelor, Rock of Love and Flavor of Love—all Princess Culture derivatives.

All the princesses wait to be *chosen*. They never do the choosing. That's a passive position to take when considering whom to marry.

Instead of conditioning girls to pick the person that's best for them, the paradigm encourages girls to wait to be chosen. Will he like me or the stepsisters? Will he choose me if the slipper fits?

That's a self-defeating way to teach girls how to pick a spouse.

No wonder there's a one-in-two divorce rate. Half the women realized they got picked by a wrong or incompatible prince.

The princesses are willing to spend the rest of their lives with someone they don't even know.

I have done my best, verbally, and by way of example and distraction, to steer Ainsley away from Princess Culture. I tell her to pick another movie or book. I tell her what's wrong with the princess's choices and assumptions about her capability to save herself. I expose her to better and more powerful characters in literature, movies and television.

I stop short of completely forbidding all princess pretend play because I don't want to make it more attractive—as the forbidden often is. I want her to be able to talk to me about anything, and obviously if I can't take a little Cinderella chat then sex will be out of the question later. I want to keep the dialogue open.

Still, for all my talk, for Halloween we dress up to be caricatures of 1980s beauty queens, and she declares herself Cinderella—same pink, frilly and pouffy thrift-store dress.

This is a very different idea of who girls and women are. I hear the argument that mothers are the biggest influence in their daughters lives—I make the argument all the time—but all evidence suggests there is no amount of magic on earth that's going to negate Disney's *girl crack* message that girls should be a b-l-e-e-p-i-n-g princess.

High School Musical 2

Everyone is talking about *High School Musical 2*, with 17.2 million viewers during the premiere. Ainsley and I watched it together.

Isn't this just *Dirty Dancing* for kids? Here's the formula:

Cute, poor kid works at a country club for the summer. He's really good friends with all the other employees. Rich girl Sharpay tries to buy his love and exclude his friends. She uses such "manipulation" as to try to get him on the college basketball team and use her family clout with the university to help him get ahead.

His friends say this: Who are you, you sell out? What about your friends? You're not the guy we thought you were.

Everything culminates in a talent show (*Dirty Dancing* anyone?) where the employees win and the evil rich girl loses. But Sharpay is okay with that and has learned her lesson.

I honestly think this is a fine, age-appropriate movie. However, I did tell my daughter that the moral of the story—rich people are evil and good kids shouldn't pursue success because they'll leave friends behind—just isn't true to life.

I, for one, wish I hadn't taken such storybook morality to heart. My issue is with the rich versus poor theme. Poor doesn't equal moral or nice. Nor does rich equal evil. Allowing our daughters

29

to think these stories are true to life or can be applied to real life situations will inevitably keep them poor. That's all I'm saying. Poor is not a future I wish on either of my children. Neither is guilt for earning a living. Certainly, I don't want to present it as an either/or choice.

As the only father figure in the movie says, "It's okay to keep your eye on the prize and go for it."

It's unfortunate the same formula films with the "poor is the moral choice" theme keep getting recycled and spoon-fed generation after generation. It leaves people, especially women, feeling conflicted when they work hard to make money.

The very least we can do, as parents, is point out the discrepancies between culture and reality.

Love Drunk: High School Musical 3

I took Ainsley and her BFF to see *High School Musical 3*.

I have a mad hot crush on Zac Efron. I don't care. No one has moved me with such theatrical gyrations and love songs since I was about Ainsley's age watching John Travolta in *Grease* for the first time.

Zac and John—two generations of the same fantasy lover. Take your judgment elsewhere. He's hot.

I thought I was too mature for fantasy lovers, and I felt great relief from the idea that romantic love of the Disney Romance brand held no attraction for me anymore. And it was liberating.

But, I left *High School Musical 3* in a state of what can only be described as *Love Drunk*.

It's like the milk drunk babies get from breast feeding, the intoxicating high some women get from reading romance trash like *Twilight*, and the drunk you get from planning your fantasy wedding, which results in Bridezilla, the lightheadedness girls get from the very first kiss ever or from fantasizing about romantic declarations of love and devotions expressed by your future one and only.

Love Drunk. Girls are prone to it.

Love Drunk would be the most wildly fun and pleasant experience in life—if men and boys weren't so chronically disappointing, often declaring such things "stupid" and adamantly refusing to play their role as gyrating, dancing, wooing, admiring, verbal and romantic leading men, thus leaving women and girls everywhere chronically disappointed in their real-life relationships. It's our modern-day love conundrum.

Nonetheless, I greatly enjoyed this unrealistic, gravely naive, and absolutely fun and wonderful film. It will earn you mega relationship capital with your girls.

On a practical note, the things I loved about what this film had to say about gender and gender roles include:

- Gabriella, female romantic lead, is selected for prestigious academic honor at Stanford. Other colleges mentioned were Yale, Berkley, University of Albuquerque and Juliard. These kids aimed high—I like that for a standard.
- Gabriella did not ignore her potential or reduce herself to stay with Troy at University of Albuquerque, nor did she dumb down to make him feel like more of a man. Gabriella took her opportunity.
- Troy, always pressured to be the jock and play football at a specific college decided on by his father, rebelled by taking theatre.
- There were actors in the movie from every ethnicity and every body type.
- The main moral of the story is that everyone has special gifts and talents and children of both genders should pursue excellence ambitiously.
- Sharpay wasn't nearly as big a B-I-T-C-H this time. Oh, she still tried to steal the show, and she thought of no one but herself, but she was much nicer about it.

It's hilarious that both *Madagascar* and *High School Musical* challenged male gender roles by making both male romantic leads performers. Hear that John Travolta, Tom Cruise and Brad Pitt? You've paved the way for boys everywhere to be able to be jocks AND thespians.

At the beginning there is a locker-room-boys-in-towels hazing scene that was so lighthearted I couldn't get upset about it.

There is potential for you to be upset about it; I tried. Couldn't muster it.

There is also a dance scene where Gabriella's little baby doll dress is frighteningly short. Know this—it never shows her panties; it only looks like it might.

I was sitting between two teenage girls and the two first and second grade girls I brought, and their excitement was highly contagious.

The girl on my right—I did not know her from Adam—was experiencing that hormonal flood of emotion we call "puberty" in our culture, and she was moved to tears and hysterical, love-drunk giggle fits for the entire movie.

Watching her emotional expressions moved me to laughter and giggles myself. I couldn't help it.

I can't tell you how much relationship capital I earned by taking Ainsley and a friend to see this fun little movie.

Coincidentally, I read about a new brand of Disney Movie in *O Magazine* this month. Abigail Disney, a niece of the late great Walt Disney, feels as ambivalent as I do about Disney Princess movies, and thus she avoided the studio her whole life.

That is until she felt compelled to tell the story of Liberia's Women who ended their civil war by threatening to take their clothes off. Read more about that in *The Rabble Rousers*.

While that was an intriguing variation on the Disney Movie, my next thought was this: How do we get Abigail Disney to give up her boycott of the family business and transform Disney's male-dominated, male-written and male-produced princess films into something we can be thrilled to saturate our daughters' brains with?

Could there be a next generation of girl-positive Disney Movies?

Hope springs anew.

Hairspray

I took my kids and my Grandma to see *Hairspray* at the dollar movie theater. What a great family flick.

There's the obvious message about race and integration. But beneath that, there is an equally good message about size and gender.

The heroine, Tracy Turnblad, is a—what am I allowed to say without pissing anyone off—*not* a size zero (not that here's anything wrong with being naturally thin).

Tracy is depicted as the hippest and most insightful and fashionable of the girls. Other girls start to cut and color their hair like hers. They imitate her dance moves and vote her Ms. Hairspray. She gets a modeling contract for a dress store. She even scores the leading man, Link Larkin (Zac Efron of *High School Musical*).

Edna Turnblad (John Travolta in a fat suit and a dress), it turns out, hasn't left the house in ten years due to embarrassment about her size. She shares that she dreamed of owning a coin-operated laundry mat, but gave that up. Nor did housewives "stay home and not work" which is how our Norman Rockwell memory likes to paint the wife of the 1960s; rather they took in other people's laundry to make ends meet. Tracy made her mom her manager and asked her to negotiate her contract. This was such a new thing for any woman, let alone one who felt her appearance wasn't even good enough to be seen in public.

"I'll teach you how to do it, Mom," Tracy tells her mother. We've been teaching our mothers how to think in new ways and challenge the status quo for a couple of generations now. I can't wait for the lessons my daughter teaches me.

The bottom line is that this is a movie with powerful female characters who reject their "proper place" in society. Tracy not only thought up and led an integration march; she risked her boyfriend to do it.

"Change isn't just going to happen for people who are different. We're going to have to *do* something to make it happen," she tells her father.

This kind of feminine power is important for girls to see.

Plus, it came with the added perk of Zac Efron. He's Ainsley's first movie star crush, and she told me she was dreaming about him last night. I have to admit, he's totally crush worthy.

My recommendation: remove a princess movie and replace it with *Hairspray*, which has great and powerful messages about a girl who created social and cultural change.

Hannah Montana: The Movie

If you want to win Mother-of-the-Year, take your kids to see *Hannah Montana: The Movie.*

I took Ainsley and her BFF on opening day, and they both loved it.

The plot, I'll warn you now, is the exact same plot of every single one of the television episodes, but evidently some people (children) don't get bored with the same plot.

Hannah Montana has a lot of career choices and must-do appearances that interfere with her alter ego, Miley's, interpersonal relationships—best friend Lily, father, brother, school—sort of like every adult woman I know, especially working mothers.

She often makes the mistake of scheduling a "Hannah Event," like the Music Awards or a save-the-town concert, and a "Miley Event," like her first date with a cute cowboy, for the exact. same. time.

Then you get to watch her run through revolving doors changing clothes and wigs—brown, blond, brown, blond, brown, blond—while she changes and confuses her roles and identities.

I could bring that back to the modern-day woman's dilemma— I'm a professional, I'm a mom, I'm a professional, I'm a mom, I wear a business suit, I wear my yoga pants with spit up on them,

I wear a business suit, I wear my yoga pants with spit up on them. Like that.

Eventually she gets busted, just as we all do.

When you get down to it, Disney is just trying to prepare young girls for the crazy, hectic and stressful insanity of being a mom and a professional—right? "Well, *you're* the one who said you wanted 'the best of both worlds,'" is often repeated in the show (and in the lives of real women).

Anywho, you can take your kids to see this, and there will be no inappropriate nudity or violence. Nothing inappropriate at all. Really.

You do, however, get to see Hannah Montana throw down with Tyra Banks over a pair of designer heels. Which isn't a female stereotype at all.

Hannah Montana Branding

Have you gotten the four-page Hannah Montana brand advertisement from Walmart?

"Maddy gets *all* the Hannah Montana stuff! She has the wigs and the microphone and sleeping bag and DVD and CD. How come she gets it, and I don't?," Ainsley complained.

Hannah Montana is a Disney Channel sitcom, and she's played by Miley Cyrus, Billy Ray Cyrus's daughter. She's a secret rock star by night and a normal girl who goes to public school by day.

Last year Hannah was on our Not Allowed to Watch List because of her tone and the dating themes. But I think we've established that Ainsley is getting her tone straight from the source—me—rather than Hannah.

I argued to allow Hannah because she keeps Ainsley (and Zack) occupied while I write.

But since the Best of Both Worlds Tour commenced, the commando marketing is starting to get to me. Have you ever seen an entire four-page ad dedicated to one celebrity brand? I can't say that I have.

Of course, Ainsley wants everything in it.

- socks
- shirts
- capris with Hannah's face on the cuffs
- electric toothbrush
- gift card
- glasses frames (Hannah doesn't wear glasses)
- purse
- guitar purse
- watch
- t-shirts
- hats
- pajamas
- sleeping bag
- plates and napkins
- Mini-Wheats cereal
- song cards
- bedding set
- throw
- Nintendo system and games
- posters
- sticker card fun pack
- paperback books
- DVDs
- CDs
- wigs in many different colors
- singing dolls
- doll paraphernalia
- electric guitar

With the concert selling out at reported one thousand dollar tickets, Hannah mania is feeling more and more like a deranged attempt to seep funds out of parents' pockets.

The lesson here is to teach girls how to resist commando marketing.

No. You don't need all that Hannah Montana stuff.

It sounds so simple, doesn't it? No. You don't need it.
I just haven't gotten a lot more creative than that.
Well, aside from my ordinary lessons on being a wise consumer.

Good-bye
Hannah Montana

ood-bye, Hannah Montana.

I'm sick and tired of hearing your bratty little attitude and disrespect come out of my daughter's mouth.

Months ago I tried to blame *myself* for my daughter's snotty tone and disrespectful banter. I tried to ban my "tone" and keep you, Hannah, as harmless entertainment.

But here's the thing: I add quality to my daughter's life whether I take a tone or not. I'm her mother, and she's definitely better off with me than she is without me. There's no question that the benefit of me outweighs the cost of my tone.

It's unfortunate, but I can't say the same about you.

It has nothing to do with your back-exposure, Miley, which I felt was a trumped-up way for the media to call yet another girl a "whore," as we know that's their hobby. I feel bad about that.

It's Hannah's mouth and Hannah's attitude. That mouth and that dialogue are being used against *me*.

My daughter thinks it's funny to imitate.

And I agree. It's funny to imitate.

But if it's a choice between *you* and *me* in my daughter's life. Well, I pick *me*. Because I add quality, and you, well, you don't. When your snotty, bratty, disrespectful banter comes out of my daughter's mouth—well, to be completely truthful, I feel like slapping her. I don't. But really, it shouldn't take so much effort to stop the impulse.

Also, you're not really age-appropriate, no matter how small you make the t-shirts or how you commando market to Kindergarteners and preschoolers.

She's listening to you talk about your "needs" and how your super-protective bodyguard is getting in the way of those needs.

Now I know your "needs" are probably to be kissed and to hold hands, though you left it vague. Too vague.

But that's too much information, and too vague, for my six-year-old daughter. And again, I didn't really like your tone when you discussed your "needs" with your dad. In fact, I thought your dad handled it poorly—like a schmuck. (While we're speaking of your parents, I have to wonder—why exactly has Disney killed off all the girls' mothers, including yours?)

So I took control of the remote. I couldn't figure out how to just block Hannah Montana, so I blocked the entire Disney Channel. Truth be told, I'm not a huge fan of your other influences, Disney, what with the snotty attitude from Zack and Cody and the Princess Culture nightmare I've had to wade through with my daughter.

So there you are, Disney Channel.

Blocked—along with the pay-per-view porn.

Bored With Being Incensed

Noah Cyrus, Miley's nine-year-old sister was photographed on a stripper pole with her friends at a nightclub before the Teen Choice Awards. Read that story on *Dlisted*.

Also in the *Dlisted* story is a new teen pop group titled "The Lolitas." You know, like the elementary-aged little girl who "made" Humbert Humbert rape and molest her in the child pornography "classic" *Lolita*.

I'm tired of being shocked and incensed that America's children are being treated in this way. Does anyone have any other ideas? I'm leaning toward social annihilation and threat of physical harm.

When I was sixteen years old, I was stark raving mad boy crazy. I was promiscuous and extremely provocative. My parents, my whole family, were fundamentally religious, and I simply could. not. be. contained. I was hypersexual. However much my parents, my religion, my school pushed for purity and abstinence, I resisted.

I wanted to attract a mate, boys, a boyfriend. I wanted to be hot. I was hot. I loved being hot. It was wildly exciting to attract boys. It was a total adrenaline rush to feel super-attractive and sexual. It was extremely stimulating to dress in a way that made my mother shudder.

At sixteen years old, Miley Cyrus's Teen Choice performance seems...on time.

But it is inappropriate, to say the least, from my current parental perspective. And it is inappropriate for my seven-year-old daughter and three-year-old son for sure.

This is why I did not sit down with my young children and partake of The Teen Choice Awards. My kids are not a teens, and they are not ready for this. I'm not ready for this.

In case you think the world has just ended because Miley Cyrus danced provocatively in front of other stark raving mad, hormonally charged teenagers—just remember, girls generally come off this type of sex-crazed high once they get married and have children. Granted, this did not prove true for Britney Spears (yet). Still, most of us tend to come to our senses during motherhood.

I still love Madonna, a love born as a young teenager watching her be powerfully provocative and sexually experimental in the '80s. Loved her then and love her now. How is this different? "Like a Virgin" and "Papa Don't Preach," anyone?

Just think of it as a Law of Attraction. It's part of biological law that sixteen-year-old girls are going to be intent on attracting attention to their sexuality. Once they've fulfilled their biological drive and reproduced, they'll see the whole mating-dance thing to be…as inappropriate as we see it now.

What's different about her sister, Noah, being photographed on a pole and her older sister, Miley's, dancing?

Noah is nine years old.

Miley is sixteen years old.

Seven years.

Miley's Photo

I'm conflicted about this.

Wasn't the media just lying in wait for the girl to screw up and cross the very fine line between contemporary and provocative?

"*Vanity Fair* wants to sell magazines," one newswoman says.

"Exactly right," another newswoman says.

"Yeah, true," I say. "But no more than you want higher viewer ratings and are deliberately competing with *Entertainment Tonight.*"

Seems everyone wants to capitalize on Miley's misstep—the news stations, the newspapers are all feeding on the story like rating-hungry wolves.

I find that is just as girl-exploitive as the actual photographs.

Miley has apologized, and so has Annie Lebowitz, who shot the photo.

TWILIGHT: FEMALE CRACK COCAINE

My much-adored cousin told me I just *had* to read *Twilight* (book one of *The Twilight Saga*) by Stephenie Meyer, which is flying off the shelves as women indulge our addiction to the love story.

In the meantime, I've been contemplating a few things like why girls and women can be so self-defeating.

Why does the battered wife stay or go back?

Why are girls willing to put up with blatant disrespect for boyfriends?

Why do women and girls tend to glamorize "giving up everything" for their husbands and children?

What is wrong with us?

Women make up 50 percent of the population, yet we have so little of the world's power. Why?

Read *Twilight*.

Edward, the beautiful vampire, tells Bella, the teenage human girl, over and over that his biggest desire is to kill her. That he can barely contain himself whenever he's around her. Her own demise only turns her on. She has zero sense of self-preservation. She "loves" him. Within the first week of meeting Edward, who immediately treats her like crap because he wants to harm her so badly he finds it difficult to resist, she gives up her friends, her studies, her father and her mother and all of her interests. Giving up everything is "worth it." (Where have I heard that line before, Mothers?)

The answer to all those questions is this: we think it's romantic. It makes us hot. It makes us linger in the bathtub or passes the time quickly on the treadmill.

The self-defeat, the sacrifice, the giving up of self is in our feminine collective dialogue, and it's like crack cocaine to us.

Women are addicted to this emotional drug that we call "Love" but which is really a lot more like unhealthy emotional psychosis.

It starts with the Disney Princess drama as toddlers and children.

But, then we grow up, and it has no effect on us our "real life." Right?

Then why is the *Twilight* series flying off the shelves?

There's no sex in the book (because he would crush her vulnerable and breakable body). But, really, is sex the most self-destructive thing girls participate in? I think not. I would hold up "Love," and our distortions of it, as the most dangerous thing to girls' confidence, their self-esteem, their sense of self, their psychological and emotional health. How many girls have sex too soon for this distortion of "Love"?

Here's the other thing that gets me about this type of literary dialogue, it's so prevalent in the collective female culture. Yet the "give up everything" theme doesn't exist in men's literature. Except when the female is doing it and most notably in porn.

How many relationships have actually self-destructed with these words, "But I gave up everything for you!" as women/girlfriends/wives declare?

"Who asked you to? Why would you do that?" men want to know. Love is not described in the same terms, nor defined by the need for women to give up so much of themselves that they no longer actually exist, in the literary consciousness of men.

Women keep acting out the same self-destructive communication patterns and the same self-sacrificing behaviors found in books like *Twilight,* and men are completely bewildered by it.

The only literature or culture in which this exchange—women giving up everything—shows up is in their pornography, where women aren't featured for "Love" as we write it, they are featured as inanimate objects for a mere moment's pleasure.

Stop this little cultural miscommunication, and you most likely increase not only the duration, but also the quality of marriage in this country.

Stop buying into this ridiculously absurd, self-defeating definition of "Love" and we might actually give our daughters a shot at healthy love, positive and fulfilling relationships and enduring marriages—ones where they get to keep their selves, their identities, their interests, their talents, their careers, their hobbies, their sense of self-respect and their physical safety.

The question is this: can we have both?

Can we have our trashy teenage vampire romance novel, where we "pretend" to give up our choices and our well-being, our life even, our families, for the "love of our life" who wants to kill us and flat out tells us that, and then live empowering strong lives?

Or do we hardwire our brains to believe that doing self-defeating things for a man is "romantic"? If our brains are hardwired this way, are we passing that down to our daughters? Especially if we allow them to indulge in this type of culture and media?

True Love Waits: Twilight

I just read "True Love Waits" by Donna Freitas in *The Wall Street Journal,* an editorial about the *Twilight* vampire romance series.

She made some good points about the *Twilight* series and the sex involved. I've read the first book of the series, and though no one "does it," the book is hot with anticipation.

Freitas argues that this book encourages girls to be abstinent and helps them understand they can have fulfilling romantic relationships while demanding respect from boys.

It's a compelling argument. In theory, it's one I'd like to hop on board with.

Don't do it. It's hot not to do it. And I remember—from being a teenager—how hot it is not to do it, just to fool around, to make him chase me. It really is much hotter not to do it. (Ironically, it's so hot not to do it that it makes you want to do it.)

Except that it doesn't account for the language in the book that struck me as exactly the same dialogue we hear from battered women and victims of teen relationship violence.

This is not a small problem when you consider that around 20 percent of our teens have experienced teen dating violence.

"He can't help his natural instinct to want to destroy Bella even though he doesn't really want to," is what Stephanie Meyers argues is an acceptable reason for Edward to want to kill and harm Bella, the heroine. It's not just acceptable; it's romantic.

Battered women and codependent women (women in relationships with addicts) use this excuse in real life as a "valid reason" to stay and take more abuse from someone who declares his "love" for her and his simultaneous inability to treat her with respect. He just can't help his natural instinct. As if it's natural and normal to want to harm your love.

The question is this: is it valid?

The reason they don't "do it" in the first *Twilight* book is that his godlike strength "would crush her fragile, delicate, vulnerable body."

Oh, and his vampire instinct makes him literally want to kill her. He wants to so badly that he can barely touch her. The smell of her makes him think "lunch," the same way I feel jerks who catcall think of us "lunch—meant for my consumption."

Hello, that's not the language of patient, abstinent, sweet and touching young love. That's the language of power and violence.

Meyers pretends Bella has power over Edward because he claims that being near her drives him out of control (wanting to kill her), that he can barely contain himself. But existing in a pretty state and smelling good is a pretty passive power.

He has *power* and *control* because he gets to choose whether to kill her or not. Lucky for her he doesn't—no matter how much she wants him to—until the third or fourth book. Bella's death was another mingling of "erotic and passionate love" meets "violence and pain." My cousin read me that part over the phone, "Isn't that great writing?" she said. "Such a powerful description."

Yeah, of battered woman syndrome—not of true love.

This is not the language I want to use to make my daughter demand respect and maintain abstinence.

This is the language that makes victims of girls and women. It makes them believe that being a victim is romantic. In real life it's not at all romantic.

It's a distortion of love, not True Love.

A man who expects me not to violate my own sense of self-preservation to win his love actually loves me. We need to stop being confused about that.

If I have to give up my self, my abilities, my life, my safety, my sense self-preservation to be with him, then that is most definitely *not* true love. Those are all red flags.

You know another connotation of the word *"Twilight"* is a distancing from feelings surrounding reality; they used to put birthing mothers into a semi-coma called "twilight sleep." This way they could participate in the labor but without awareness or feeling.

Not my idea of healthy love.

I had to learn these lessons the hard way. God willing my daughter won't have to.

Should most of the issues in this series, or any of the red flag language, come up for Ainsley I hope her first and only instinct is to *run for her life and never look back.*

Teen Girls Aren't As Stupid As I Thought

Teen girls aren't as stupid as I thought. I know, this is a totally pro-girl website. That doesn't meant I think girls are always the smartest. Sometimes—especially when boys and men are involved—girls can be quite stupid. Me included. Hell, historically, me mostly.

I've been subbing at the high school and junior high this year. It's pretty fun. I adore teenagers. I'm a freak like that. I'll take a classroom of teens over a gaggle of snotty toddlers that want to cuddle with me any day.

Their regular teacher warned me that this class was really, really bad and that they couldn't be trusted not to talk if I even let them whisper, and she wanted names of anyone who uttered so much as a whisper, and she would duly punish them.

Uh, OK.

The whole not talking thing struck me as stupid when I was in junior high. It still does.

I went back to reading the third book in the *Twilight* series, *Eclipse*. What I won't do for *The Girl Revolution*, caught off guard with nothing to read, with access to a junior high library.

If you've been here before you know that I hate the *Twilight* series because I think Bella is the stupidest girl character on the

Planet Earth. But whatever, at least girls are reading. Who cares if they're reading training material for being a battered girlfriend?

That teacher was so right. As soon as the girls saw what I was reading, they started talking about *Twilight*. This is, after all, *the* girl-culture phenomenon of their time. They couldn't escape it if they wanted to. Everyone's talking about it; everyone has seen the movies, read the books, bought the branded accessories and school supplies.

"Bella is so stupid!" one girl said.

"Really? How so?" I asked, totally shocked.

"She wants to die. Don't you think that's stupid?" they said.

"Yeah, I think it's stupid, but I thought girls thought it was romantic," I said.

"No, she's totally stupid. She goes for Edward and he's totally ugly!" they said.

"In the book, he's not ugly, he's the most beautiful man in entire history of mankind, well, vampirekind!" I argued.

"In the movie, he's ugly and pasty. Jacob is sooo hot!" they declared.

One girl pulled out a photo of Jacob. He's hot.

"So, you don't think it's romantic to give up everything and die for a boy?" I asked.

"No way! I don't want to die! Why would you want to die? Would you want to die with an ugly man?" they asked.

"I hate to break it to you, but most of you will probably die with ugly men. Look around, Ladies, this is as good as boys get. Eventually they are old and bald and pot-bellied," I said. I'm sorry I can't help myself. The truth pops out of my mouth before I can stop it sometimes.

They looked around, shocked, and laughed.

One of the boys said something like, "*Twilight* is so stupid."

To which I responded, "Smart boys will read it so they know what girls want. Otherwise they'll constantly be wondering how come they disappoint their girlfriends."

"Seriously, you don't want to give up your whole life, your whole family, your ability to have children, college, careers and all that for a boy?" I asked them. I thought perhaps I might cry with relief.

"No way! Besides, she should have gone with Jacob; he's way hotter," they said.

That settles it. There is hope for the future of girls in spite of trashy-romance-novels-turned-propaganda-for-eternal-marriage.

In fact, now that I think about it, it makes those girls smarter than lots of women I know. At least for now, while it remains hypothetical.

Gossip Girl
and Date Rape

I tuned into *Gossip Girl* to see what it was about.

The new definition of glamorous includes editing a rape scene and an act of consensual (yet inappropriate drunken sex) with the intent to blur the distinction between rape and consent. The viewer was asked to be not only confused, but aroused, by the violent attack of a girl, as the producer took slices of the rape scene and slices of the consensual sex and flashed them back and forth rapidly with a strobe effect. Flash of hand on bare leg, leaving the viewer to wonder is it a rapists hand or a lover's hand? It's presented in such a way as to make rape seem provocative. Does she really mean "No" or does she mean "Yes"? After all, she's obviously not a virgin.

Unfortunately, in real life the girl is not this confused when she is attacked. Here's the difference, in one situation she's saying *no*, and in the other situation she's saying *yes*.

The rapist in the scene is a high school boy who suffers no consequences and is not confused about his actions. He knows he will get away with it, considers it a fun and exciting game, and proceeds to seek out and attempt to rape a freshman. "Is that a freshman? I like freshmen, they're so 'fresh,'" goes the dialogue. The portrayal of her rape is that she obviously deserves such treatment because she's foolish enough to go to a party with the cool kids and wear a pretty dress; shouldn't she know better? The only way she gets out of the situation is by emergency texting her brother who saves the day.

How do all the other high school girls react? Isn't this great gossip?

Is this the new standard of normal? I kept hoping I was confused, but really there was nothing mysterious about the message: "Rape of high school girls is *hot*! Even for other girls and the rape-victim herself."

The "new" CWTV has gone from innocent, sweet Gilmore Girls into the depraved child pornography genre in one season. If the consumer accepts this as the new normal, there are wide-range consequences for the sexualization of girls. Dating violence is a real problem; one in five girls is a victim of it. And I believe producers of this show are intentionally perpetuating the problem because it's getting them off. Controversy is a great way to drive up ratings.

Are we asked to believe that this is a reflection of reality? And if this is reality, why are they asking us to be aroused by it instead of outraged and disgusted by it?

As a consumer, and as a user of and advocate of free speech, as the mother of a girl and as a female myself, I encourage all advertisers to withdraw themselves from supporting the intentional blurring of rape/consent boundaries on *Gossip Girl*. Violence against women and rape of girls cannot become mainstream entertainment. This is not in the best interest of girls. This is not in the best interest of boys who date girls. This is in the best interests of NAMBLA and pedophiles and sex offenders. This is in the best interest of pornographers who like to photograph the violation of girls and encourage the consumption of girls as pure entertainment. But there is no way in which this kind of misogynistic violence for entertainment purposes can be construed as in any girl's best interest.

Rape is rape, and it's never fun for its victim. It's never funny, and no one should be confused by the glamorous presentation of it on *Gossip Girl*.

Avatar is Art: Powerful Female Characters

*Y*esterday was one of those rare days when I witnessed a staggering work of genius.

Of course I mean James Cameron's *Avatar*. It is epic.

In *The Girl Revolution* terms, it was startlingly beautiful with a mixture of female roles any parent should be proud to expose their daughters to: The Navi female lead was attractive but not hypersexual; instead she was a warrior and hunter and in line to be the next village spiritual leader. The head human scientist was science fiction genre queen, Sigourney Weaver. The human female supporting actress was a fighter pilot. The village spiritual leader was a wise and holy matriarch.

The typical female film archetypes are nowhere to be found in this epic film. The village whore was not cast, the promiscuous girl was not doing it with the football player so the audience could catch a glimpse of her boobs, the dumb blond was not featured, the submissive wife was nowhere to be found, the powerless and trapped beauty in need of saving is missing, and my friends, there was not a single evil stepmother or conniving man stealer.

The sexuality of the film was authentic. By this I mean there was no gratuitous ogling, fondling, crass, boys-will-be-boys, everyone-just-wants-to-get-laid, casual-sex-is-fun, porno-inspired, beer-commercial-craptastic, look-at-the-plastic DDDs, Oh-Edward-I-want-to-damn-my-soul-and-die-to-spend-eternity-with-you, prince-come-save-me-for-I-am-helpless "romantic" scenarios.

There was a singular sex/romance scene in the entire drama, in which the male and female leads chose each other after several months of non-sexual intimacy and spiritually joined together at the Navi's holiest temple. The scene was not graphic nor pornographic, but was very loving and intimate. It ended with the words, "We are mated for life."

As a creative-type myself, it was a sheer pleasure to experience the film. I consider it of high honor to witness an artist's work of creative genius. Creative energy that is poured out in a spiritual way, as in this film, is even better. I had read in a New Yorker article about Cameron's visualizing the Navi and the Pandora world since the 1970s, and my interest was piqued. My main attraction to the film was to see what thirty years of meditating, expanding, working on idea would culminate in. The sheer scale of the film is tantalizing. The attention to detail is intimidating. The technology he invented to make the film is a creation in high-tech genius. The visual beauty is so great that several times I gasped in awe and wonder.

The film is so surreal you can taste it, smell it, touch it. There is a palpable and quite lovely energy to the film one can absorb if one is so inclined. I am.

Jeremy, my husband, and I are debating whether to allow Ainsley to see it. I want to expose her to creative and inspiring genius while it's in the theaters, with the 3D glasses for full effect. DVD will not do this film justice. It will be like turning a pop-up book into a flat postcard. *Avatar* will be this generation's Star Wars. I believe it will be culturally significant, become part of the lexicon of world culture, weave its way into our speech and casual conversations, develop a following of people who parade around in blue and have Navi conventions, and change Halloween costumes forever. I don't want her to miss it. It will be culturally significant in a way that someone who forgoes the experience will be missing cues, comments and humor. I don't want her to miss an opportunity to witness creative genius. *Avatar* is Art—rare, precious and inspiring.

Jeremy disagrees. He feels it is too emotionally intense for an eight-year-old. He feels the themes are rather mature, the emotions run extremely high, and it will be overwhelming or frightening for her.

BATTERED WOMEN, TIME TO LEAVE

According to the US Justice Department, 30 percent of women are beaten by a significant other at one time or another.

This is an issue very close to my heart, as I was a battered girlfriend for two years, between fourteen and sixteen years old, so I actually know why these women stay. I also know how much courage it takes to leave.

In college, when a boyfriend started getting abusive, I left quickly. But then he stalked me for months, and finally the police were going to put him away for two years. I begged them not to. I knew the last thing I needed was for that man to plot my murder for two years. The court required him to leave the state immediately. He was not allowed to return for two years, or else he would go to prison.

Yesterday on *Oprah*, the battered woman's son who witnessed everything expressed the key to both his mother's and my personal experience : *do not stay!*

Many women stay because of their children. I can understand the thinking behind this. You don't want your children to come from a broken home. You don't want to put them through a divorce. You don't want the stigma.

You are so confused that you think he will change. That if you do enough things right, he will stop his abusive behavior. You believe him when he says, "You make me hit you; if you cleaned the house like you were supposed to, then I wouldn't have to hit you."

You believe him because you want to believe you can somehow make him stop by being exactly what he wants you to be. You believe him because this is logic you use on your kids, and you are telling the truth, "If you cleaned your room yesterday, you wouldn't be grounded." You want him to be telling the truth, but he's not.

You believe, in your heart, that you deserve abuse because you are a terrible person. You are a whore, a slut, a horrible mother, a bad cook, a terrible housekeeper, stupid, idiotic, moronic—whatever names he chooses to call you. The worst my ex-boyfriend would call me was "used meat." After all, who wants a girl who's not a virgin anymore? You have been listening to his berating of yourself for so long that you believe every word of it is true. That's why you stay. You stay because you think no one else would want you, and you're not strong enough to stand on your own. This is emotional terrorism, and every word he says is untrue.

To get out, you need to repeat all the good and wonderful and true qualities to yourself over and over and over until you believe them enough to go. You need to quietly work your self-worth up through praise of self until you no longer believe his lies about you.

Your daughter, when she hears his opinion of you over and over and sees him hit you, comes to believe these things, not only about you, but also about herself. If you are a terrible slut, then she is a terrible slut. If you deserve to be hit, then she does as well. It doesn't matter if she is three or fourteen, the result will be that she will find someone who hits her or emotionally terrorizes her, and she will call it love.

You cannot raise an empowered girl if you are staying in an abusive relationship. It is an unequivocal impossibility.

Battered women, I know it's hard to feel that you are worth leaving him. But it's not as hard to feel that your children are worth leaving for. And they are.

The last bit of advice is not to leave without a plan. I left without a plan twice. Frankly, it was scary. Both times the man stalked me, attacked me in public, stole my mail, called my job so many times I got fired, harassed my friends, broke into my house, etc.

You are strong enough to make it on your own.

You are good enough to find someone else.

You are smart enough to find your way out of this.

You are a wonderful person who deserves to be free of abuse.

DATING VIOLENCE

In Texas, almost 188,000 incidents of domestic violence occurred during 2005, and more than 330,000 rapes occur every year, according to Gov. Rick Perry's office.

It starts with the girls and boys. Intimate violence is not a problem that develops when healthy adults get together.

Both the victim and the offender attribute responsibility for dating violence to the victim. The majority of both girls and boys cite the girl's appearance, the girl's personality, the girl's provocation, the girl's communication style, the girl's need for affection or the girl's peer group influence as the cause of intimate partner violence.

Prevalence and Frequency

- Females aged sixteen to twenty-four are the most vulnerable to intimate partner violence, suffering at a rate of three times the national average.
- Both males and females report being victims of dating violence. However, boys injure girls more severely and frequently.
- One in five female high school students report being abused by an intimate partner.
- 22 percent of all homicides of females between sixteen and nineteen were committed by their intimate partner.
- Half of adult sex-offenders admit their first violent offense occurred before age eighteen.
- Half of reported date rape happens to teenagers.

- Teens who experience partner violence are at increased risk for unhealthy eating behaviors, sexually risky behaviors, pregnancy, suicide, and substance abuse.

Parental Awareness

- 81 percent of parents say dating violence is not an issue or they don't know if it is.
- 54 percent of parents have never discussed it with their kids.

Teen Awareness

- 33 percent of teens have witnessed a dating violence incident.
- 20 percent of male students say they have witnessed a friend hitting his girlfriend.
- 39 percent of females report that whether a person is trying to control his partner is a common topic of conversation.
- 57 percent say they know someone who has been verbally, physically or sexually abusive in a dating relationship.
- 45 percent of girls say they know someone who has been pressured into intercourse or oral sex.
- One in three teens say they know someone who has been punched, hit, kicked or slapped by their dating partner.

Reporting

- Among females, 83 percent said they would confide in a friend. Only 7 percent said they would tell the police.
- 33 percent of teens who have been the victim of abuse never told anyone.

The Offender

- Out of 1,600 teen sex offenders, only 33 percent said sex was an expression of caring and love.
- 25 percent said it was about power and control.
- 9.4 percent said it was a way to dissipate anger.
- 8.4 percent said it was a method of punishment.

Contributing Factors

- One study found a high correlation between teen-mothers being abuse by their partners within 3 months after the birth of the baby.

- 77 percent of female and 67 percent of male high school students endorse some form of sexual coercion such as unwanted touching, kissing, hugging, genital contact and sexual intercourse.
- Male peer support for violence against women is a constant predictor of violence against dating partners.
- 50 percent of victims of dating violence report being suicidal, compared with 12 percent of non-abused girls and 4.5 percent of non-abused boys.

Source: American Bar Association (2006): National Teen Dating Violence Prevention Initiative, http://www.clothesline-project.org/teendatingviolencefacts.pdf

Child Molesters' Weapon of Choice: I Love You!

"Oprah's Conversation with Child Molesters," (Feb. 8, 2010) included important insights into the weapon of child molesters.

There were four molesters who confessed a great deal: one old man who molested a five-year-old little girl who loved him enough to call him Grandpa; one adult man who used the words "I love you" to rape four teenagers; one boy/man who used his younger cousin's parental distance to manipulate, molest and rape her for nearly a decade; and one father who fantasized about performing oral sex on his twelve-year-old daughter until he began touching her in her sleep in real life.

The common themes among these molesters were that their fantasies came first. They all said it stemmed from fantasy first. They all used their victim's love for them and trust in them to manipulate them. They all lied to themselves about what they were doing, making them excellent liars to the girls' parents.

When Oprah asked one man if he thought about what he had done to his victim, he responded poignantly, "I killed who she would have been."

Talking to Kids about Love

Oprah's discussion with sex offenders got me thinking.

Hopefully it had this effect on you.

Stranger Danger is...well, it's very unlikely that harm will come from a stranger. In fact in less than 10 percent of all cases of rape, molestation and battery of girls and women is the culprit a stranger.

So how do parents walk the fine line between protecting their children from friends and family without inhibiting all close relationships with men?

Certainly one can see that being hyper-vigilant and suspicious of all male contact will have a damaging effect on girls and their future, appropriate, grown-up relationships.

Still...no one wants to risk allowing a perpetrator free access to their daughters just because they have the title Uncle, Grandpa or Cousin.

The weapon of choice for all four men on *Oprah* was Love Distortion in some form.

If you love me...you'll let me touch, lick or have sex with you.

If you love me...you won't tell.

I love you more than your parents do. No one understands or loves you like I do.

I love you so much that I want to do these "loving" things with you.

When it comes down to it, this is my primary complaint with the Disney Princess Culture and the *Twilight* series. They distort what love looks like, what it should feel like, and they misrepresent the cues and signals girls should be looking for.

Take Ariel, who silences herself and gives up her family—she's the perfect statutory rape victim, really. She's the ultimate battered girlfriend. Isolation is a perpetrator's method, and silencing his victim is how he gets her to give up her own power.

Or Belle. She's kidnapped and falls in love with her own abuser. Turns him into a prince even. Um, held against your will should not be confused as a signal of "love," but a signal of abuse. Yet by the age of three or four, girls are inundated with the idea that kidnapping could be a very romantic scenario. Is it really a mystery why girls get confused when someone they love or someone who professes to love them while harming them touches them inappropriately? The promise of The Beast Turned Prince is what every battered girlfriend and wife believes in.

Then there's Edward of the *Twilight* series, whose main desire is to destroy Bella. It's his instinct; he can't help it, just like batterers claim. All the erotic scenes describe in great detail how it would feel to her and to him for him to crush her fragile lovely body, for him to drain her of her life's blood. And it made girls and women hot. We have a whole generation of girls who are now turned on by their own physical destruction and earthly demise. She begs him to kill her, and he just won't do it...until what? Book three or four? There is also that deathly-erotic description in book two about her near-death. Why, I have to ask, is it a turn-on for a guy to want to destroy you? Why are we training daughters to be desperate to give up their lives, futures, relationships with parents and friends, college, future jobs, and children for pretty boys or vampires?

As a survivor of dating violence myself, I can attest that the language of a violent boyfriend, and the lies I told myself about his behavior, is almost verbatim the dialogue of Edward the death-worthy vampire and his suicidal girlfriend Bella.

Her story—our story—feeds the rapists, child molesters, girl-friend and wife batterers. The fairytales we read to our daughters at night groom them to believe in a really distorted and danger-ous definition of Love.

When Oprah does a wife-battering episode, she is known to say, "Love doesn't hurt." Yet in all the above examples, we've, as a culture, romanticized a distorted version of love that does hurt. We glamorize the pain, make it romantic and sexualize it until it turns us on.

It would be so much smarter and beneficial to tell our daugh-ters other, healthier things about love. Our sons, too—so they don't get confused and start hurting their girlfriends in a screwed up attempt to be a murderer/protector like Edward or an ass-hole who promises to change like The Beast.

Just yesterday a group of junior high boys told me they pantsed a girl, and that it wasn't wrong or sexual assault because she liked it. Gee, I wonder where boys might get the idea that girls like it when boys hurt them? Could it be our infatuation with the vic-timization in princess stories and *Twilight?*

It may seem obvious, but we need to talk to our kids about fundamental things like, "What is love? What does it really feel like? How will they really know it's True Love? What are the cues of boys who truly care about girls? What cues should boys put out when he cares about a girl? When a girl falls in love, what kinds of feelings can she really expect to feel?"

1 Corinthians 13:4 describes Love: " Love is patient. Love is kind. It does not envy. It does not boast. It is not proud."

Other translations include "Love isn't jealous. It doesn't sing its own praises. It isn't arrogant."

This is key, because many, many abusive boys and men use jealousy and arrogance to put girls on the defensive and make them feel they "deserve" to be beaten or raped. They fly into jeal-ous rages and become arrogantly possessive of their girlfriends, not allowing them to see friends or family.

I would encourage parents to sit down and think about what Love feels like to them. Does it feel like meaningful sacrifice, like methodical work, like a warm bed, like a soft place to land, like a physical rhythm or a shelter from a storm? Does it feel different from sexual arousal, different from primitive adolescent hormones, different from a new infatuation? How is it different? Then talk about it to both sons and daughters.

Love is not Disney. Love is not *Twilight*. Love is not *Gossip Girl*. Do our kids even know that?

Rihanna, You Make Me Feel ...

Rihanna, twenty-year-old music star, was beaten by her famous boyfriend Chris Brown. Evidently, it's happened four times before and Rihanna asked the judge *not* order Chris Brown to stay away from her. Since the beating, it's been said—and I heard this on Ryan Seacrest's radio show, so it might be true—that Rihanna and Chris Brown were in a studio yesterday recording a duet.

Oprah had this to say to Rihanna and other battered girls and women, "Love doesn't hurt. If he hit you once he will hit you again."

True that. But what do we tell our kids? Kids who might actually look up to the singer and her boyfriend? Who previously fantasized in their bedrooms at night, "If only I could find a true love like Rihanna and Chris Brown." Yeah, those kids are out there. Bad enough that he beat her. Worse that she's staying.

First it's important to understand why Rihanna would participate in this type of insanity.

Yes. She's participating. Yes. It's insanity.

She believes, as nearly all battered women and girlfriends do, that she has caused Chris Brown's feelings. When Chris Brown feels in love and passionately lovey dovey and head-over-heels for her, she believes it's because she was good enough, pretty enough, nice enough, lovable enough, wonderful enough. That's her goal. To make Chris Brown love her.

Our Love Culture teaches girls that they can change and control the feelings of men. We often believe we can make them love us.

How many times have we heard or said the phrase, "You make me feel…?"

Belle ultimately changes the Beast by being beautiful and wonderful and clever enough to make him feel love. The whole fairytale centers around the idea that Belle can change, and therefore control, the Beast's feelings if she's just good enough, pretty enough, loving enough and wonderful enough.

The same distorted thinking is in the wildly popular *Twilight* series. Bella is so stunningly beautiful, clever and all-around wonderful that she makes vampire boyfriend Edward Cullin resist his natural temptation to destroy her. Throughout the books, we're transfixed, and even turned on and aroused by, imagery of Edward Cullen's overwhelming desire to crush her fragile and delicate, hot body, which is why the couple doesn't cave into sex.

This is all well and good, except that we have a Love Culture where around 30 percent of teenage girls and adult women are being battered by their love interest.

The sane thing for a woman or girl to do when someone hits her is to say, "F#$& you! You are on your way out the door, never, ever to return."

Instead the mental Love Distortion of Rihanna and nearly all other battered women and girls says, "If I didn't make him angry, he wouldn't hit me. If I did what he wanted me to do when he wanted me to do it, he wouldn't hit me. If I just try harder, I can change him from a beast into the loving boyfriend I imagine. If I'm just good enough, nice enough, pretty enough, sexy enough, then he'll resist his entirely natural male urge to destroy, kill or berate me. I'll just try harder and give him another chance."

Chris Brown agrees. Nearly all abusive men and boys agree with their beaten-up girlfriends and wives, "She's causing the violence because she's making me angry."

The fundamental problem with Rihanna's thinking is that women do not and cannot control men's feelings.

We never could.

We never can.

Ever.

Feelings originate with the person feeling them. They do not come from outside of us.

The only person who can control one's violently angry feelings is the person feeling the violently angry feelings. For a batterer to stop beating his girlfriend or wife, he has to take responsibility for and learn to control his own feelings. For a battered woman or girl to leave her abuser, she has to hold him responsible for his feelings and stop trying to change or control his feelings with her behavior.

This almost never happens while a couple stays together. Not never. But almost never. In fact, what generally happens is that he becomes worse and worse at controlling his violently angry feelings, and sometimes he kills her.

Why?

They both believe it's her fault. They both believe she's causing it. They would have to both agree that it's his fault and hold him accountable for it to change. How often do two insane people reach a clarity of thinking at the same time, in the same relationship, when it's already gotten to the point of physical violence? Almost never.

This is why in many progressive and right-thinking states the court refuses to give battered women an option of not prosecuting or of having immediate contact with their abuser. They realize that the victim's thinking is as distorted as that abuser's.

There is not a lot we can do about Rihanna. She's deep in Love Distortion, a form of insanity clinically referred to as Battered Woman Syndrome or Co-dependence. Hopefully, she'll find her inner Tina Turner or Madonna and kick Chris Brown to the curb. (Ike who? Congratulations on your new Oscar, Sean Penn.)

As parents, counselors, educators we do have a lot of power to teach both our daughters and our sons these fundamental lessons for prevention:

You are responsible for your feelings.

You are responsible for how you behave.

You cannot control other people or their feelings.

Other people cannot make you feel anything.

We can also use Rihanna and Chris Brown as a teachable moment by repeating Oprah's advice to our girls—just in case they fall for the wrong guy: Love doesn't hurt. If he hits you once he will hit you again.

Reproductive Coercion in Teens

Newsweek (Jan. 26, 2010 issue) has an article about a phenomenon called Reproductive Coercion.

Essentially, the male in the relationship is coercing the female to become pregnant so he can control her forever, through the child. After the baby, he reasons, he'll be able to control her forever. Her odds of leaving him to find another man lessen, and he will have more control over the rest of her life. Having a baby only strengthens her resolve to stay in a dangerous relationship.

New research suggests that we find reproductive coercion in the same relationships as physical and emotional abuse. A man's desire to control his partner is the same motivator as all other forms of abuse, and one of the mechanisms for controlling his partner is trying to get her pregnant.

He may insist she not use birth control, monitor her menstrual cycle, flush birth control pills down the toilet, forbid her from seeing a doctor or going to a family planning clinic, and refuse to use a condom or poke a hole in one.

Like domestic and dating violence, the rate of reproductive coercion for teenage girls mirrors the rate for adult women.

The difference being that teenage girls have little experience with relationships and often don't know that what is happening to them is wrong, dangerous, controlling or abusive.

The boundary between reproductive coercion and relationship violence—and whether there is, in fact, a boundary at all—is a difficult issue for health-care providers to address. In some cases, it can fit a spectrum of other abusive behaviors, from threatening to physical violence, that create an imbalance in a relationship's power dynamic.

"Just like violence, it's a power thing," says Leslie Walker, chief of adolescent medicine at Seattle Children's Hospital, in the Newsweek article. She state she has seen patients whose boyfriends monitor their periods to ensure they're not taking Depo-Provera contraceptive shots (which often cause women to skip their period). "The man is taking away a woman's power to decide she's not going to have a child."

Still, the line is unclear. Elizabeth Miller, an assistant professor of pediatrics at University of California, Davis, for example, would be hesitant to categorize reproductive coercion as a form of partner violence, since many states have laws mandating reporting of such incidents. "I'm not sure that a young woman telling me that her partner flushed her birth control down the toilet necessitates me reporting that to the authorities," says Miller. In these situations, Miller has two concerns: getting the teenager onto a birth control she can hide from her partner (possibly Depo-Prevera shots, which last three months and are administered at a doctor's office) and building a relationship with the patient to explore the possibility of ending the relationship. "What we hear from domestic violence survivors is they don't like being told they have to leave a relationship," says Miller. "So instead of saying, 'This is an abusive relationship,' our counseling is very much focused on having them explain how this affects their health."

In every situation, every abusive relationship is about control.

The best prevention is to talk with your daughter about her right and responsibility to control her own body, her own mind, her own choices, her own life, her own future, her own decisions, her own reproductive system, her own friends, her own job, etc.

To control ourselves is our inherent birthright.

SHE LIKED IT

The other day a group of junior high boys were laughing about having pantsed a girl.

One of them had pulled her pants down, and it was extra-hilarious that she was wearing a thong.

I told them that was actually the criminal offense of sexual assault. I told them if I were the principal, I would have them prosecuted in criminal court for doing that.

"But she liked it!" they told me.

"No she didn't," I told them. "Girls don't like it when boys rip their clothes off without their consent."

"Yes, she liked it!" they insisted.

I told them if I were principal I'd have them sent to detention for saying something so stupid.

Gee, I wonder where boys might get the idea that girls might like it?

Could it be the same places, stories where girls get the idea that it's hot for boys to harm them, that it's a natural turn-on for boys to want to destroy them, silence them, isolate them, give up their futures?

Stories like *Twilight, Beauty and the Beast, The Little Mermaid?*

It's necessary to say: It's not sane to love someone who treats you poorly, hurts you or threatens to hurt you or humiliates you in public. It's not hot to mix sex and violence. Violence against yourself or against a girl you like is not a turn on. It is not sane to love your abuser. It is not sane to abuse someone you love.

It's fundamental.

But, I think it's come to this, parents need to repeat these messages to both boys and girls.

The Girl Revolution: Forty Days of Love.

I'm encouraging you to join in *The Girl Revolution* in Forty Days of Love.

Spend forty days talking to your kids about what love is (and what it isn't) and showing them you love them.

Some ideas might include:

- Read Disney's Princess stories and talk to both girls and boys about what you wish those princesses had done.

Perhaps express to your daughter that you don't think it's romantic to give up her voice like Ariel or fall in love with a kidnapper or abusive boyfriend like Belle.

- Talk about *Twilight* and explaining that girls usually don't "pass out" from the passion of a kiss, and it's definitely not romantic if her boyfriend's "natural" instinct is to kill her. Explain that there's a difference between a romance novel and real life, and in real life you hope she keeps her dreams, educational goals, family attachments, and well... her mortal soul, and doesn't abandon them for a boy.

- Outline exactly what kinds of touching are not appropriate from relatives, friends, and boys. Explain to her that some people are bad and unfortunately and inappropriately attracted to children. Tell her their trick: they tell little girls it's okay to touch them because they love them. But girls should not believe them. If they ever hear that from someone they will know that person is a liar and trying to trick them and hurt them. This goes for Grandpa, Dad, Cousin, Uncle, Friend, Mom, Grandma, Aunt, *everyone.*

- Talk about how she'll know if a boy is right for her. Does he share the same faith, have a work ethic, write her romantic notes? There's nothing wrong with telling girls what kind of boy you hope to see her with.

- Talk to her about self-defense and some of the ways boys tried to pressure you to sexually experiment and some of the ways she can resist.

- Ask her about love and what she hopes for her future. What boys does she think are cute and why? How do boys show girls they like them at her school?

- Talk about different kinds of relationships: parents, siblings, friends, romantic partners. How can she get better at love, and how can you love her better?

- Talking about what her Love Language is. What makes her feel most loved? What makes her feel unloved? Share your experiences with her. Listen.

Who's in?

Copyright Images

Miley Photo, Image Taken from Gawker.com, Copyright Unknown

Noah Cyrus Pole Photo, Image taken from DListed.com, Copyright Unknown

All other images copyright, Tracee Sioux

BACK BLURBS

In *Love Distortion: Belle, Battered Codependent and Other Love Stories,* Tracee Sioux, creator of *The Girl Revolution* (www.thegirlrevolution.com), examines the correlation between fairytales and love stories of today's popular culture, the companies who profit from them and the real-world problems girls potentially face when they grow up and try to translate the messages from these stories into healthy romantic relationships.

Quotes about the book and author

"Tracee Sioux is a gifted writer and social observer who is keenly attuned to the serious self-image and confidence issues faced today by girls and young women. In *Love Stories We Tell Our Girls,* Tracee provides today's mothers and daughters with effective tools in combating the skewed and unrealistic portrayal of females by our society in general and by today's media in particular. As the mother of a pre-teen daughter, I know full well the challenges faced by parents today in raising confident and empowered girls. *Love Stories We Tell Our Daughters* is a must-read for any parent who wants to raise a girl to know that, regardless of what she sees and hears in the media, she is strong, smart and powerful, and much more than the sum of her looks."

– Joanne C. Bamberger, Author of *Mothers of Intention: How Women & Social Media Are Revolutionizing Politics in America* (Bright Sky Press, 2011)

"Part mindset, part movement, *The Girl Revolution* is a mighty ally with Shaping Youth in reversing narrowcast cues served to our girls daily through media and pop culture.

Founder Tracee Sioux wields her writer's pen with wit, heart and purpose to not only shield girls from gender stereotypes, but to arm them with confidence, leadership and sabers of personal truth, so they can slay through the prickly twisted web of deception themselves. Brava! Onward!"

– Amy Jussel, Executive Director of ShapingYouth.org

"I'm not sure how I ended up stepping into *The Girl Revolution* world, but what kept me there was Tracee's vision and her ability to put into action the amazing concept of growing your girls with a purpose, plus of course, empowering them in this world that we live in. I was not raised to vibrate or even resonate with power. Power was something generally male and perhaps not even human, but only left to divine beings or superheroes.

Had I been able to recognize and believe in my own power, which is a girl's birthright after all, I may have avoided some big pitfalls and lots of heartache due to misconceived notions of my role as a woman for myself and within my relationships.

Choose to step into *The Girl Revolution*. Our girls' future is counting on it!"

– Elsie Escobar, ElsiesYogaKula.com

"We all want a better world for our daughters, but Tracee is actually talking about what that would look like. I love her fierce spirit, her humor, her passion and her sharply observed insights. Bring on this revolution."

– Anna Kunnecke, Martha Beck Life Coach, Sitatmytable.com